What Did Jesus Do?

Stories about
Obedience & Friendship

MARY MANZ SIMON
ILLUSTRATED BY ANNE KENNEDY

Thomas Nelson, Inc.

Nashville

For Angela Michelle Simon, Psalm 89:1
—Mary Manz Simon

For Mom, a "big soul,"
from Annie, a "little soul"

Text copyright © 1998 by Mary Manz Simon
Illustrations copyright © 1998 by Anne Kennedy

Published in Nashville, Tennessee, by Tommy Nelson™, a division of Thomas Nelson, Inc.
Managing Editor: Laura Minchew; Editor: Tama Fortner

Scripture quotations are from The Holy Bible, New Century Version, copyright © 1987, 1988, 1991 by Word Publishing, Nashville, Tennessee. Used by permission.

Library of Congress Cataloging-in-Publication Data

Simon, Mary Manz, 1948–
    What did Jesus do? : Stories about obedience and friendship / Mary Manz Simon ; illustrated by Anne Kennedy.
        p.   cm.
    Summary: Relates two stories dealing with contemporary problems, then presents flashbacks to biblical times to see what Jesus did in similar situations.
    ISBN 0-8499-5856-3
    1. Obedience—Religious aspects—Christianity—Juvenile literature. 2. Friendship—Religious aspects—Christianity—Juvenile literature. 3. Bible stories, English—N.T. Gospels. [1. Obedience—Religious aspects—Christianity. 2. Friendship—Religious aspects—Christianity. 3. Bible stories—N.T. 4. Christian life.] I. Kennedy, Anne, 1955– ill. II. Title.
BV4647.02S56   1998
242'.62—DC21   98-7248
                                                                                                CIP
                                                                                                 AC

Printed in the United States of America
99 00 01 02 03 WCV 9 8 7 6 5 4 3 2

To the Adult

As an educator and mother of three, I care deeply about helping children develop a set of core values.

Many adults and older children embrace the "What would Jesus do?" concept. But developmentally, because young children cannot mentally change places with someone else, they can't think how someone else would respond in a specific instance. As a result, the WWJD phenomenon has had minimal impact on younger children.

However, young children copy and personally internalize behaviors modeled for them. That's why the book you hold in your hands illustrates what Jesus actually did in situations similar to those that children face every day. By looking at what Jesus did, even young children can learn to look to Him for answers to problems today.

Dr. Mary Manz Simon

Playing by the Rules

A Story about Obedience

Cole leaned over to look at the clock. Only 4:26? It felt like he'd been practicing more than 11 minutes.

"Hey, Cole, done yet?" a voice drifted in through the open window.

Grateful for an excuse to leave the piano, Cole scooted off the bench. "I've got to practice until 4:45," he answered.

"But your mom isn't home," Jason said. "She'll never know."

Cole looked at the clock again. 4:28. The house rule was clear: Practicing piano came before playing with friends. Making up his mind to break the rule, he grabbed his glove and cap.

Cole sailed out the back door.

"You practiced fast today," Kate said, flipping the ball into the air.

Half an hour later, a familiar voice called, "Hey, team."

"Hi, Mom," Cole answered, without taking his eyes off the ball.

"Sorry kids, but the ballpark is closing for today," said his mom.

"See ya," Cole yelled to his friends. He swung on the gate to close it, then went inside for a drink.

"Cole, Mrs. Palmer must have phoned while you were outside," his mom said. "I saved the message for you."

"Thanks," he said between large slurps.

The smooth voice of Mrs. Palmer drifted into the room.

"You've practiced so faithfully, Cole, that I've chosen you to open next week's recital," the recorded voice played back. "Congratulations!"

Cole's shoulders slumped.

"Practiced so faithfully . . ." he groaned. The phrase bounced around in his head all evening. What was that story in the Bible about obedience?

"I'm going fishing," Peter announced.

John, Thomas, and some of Jesus' other disciples climbed into the boat after Peter. It seemed like a good night for fishing. Again and again, the men threw out their nets. Again and again, they hauled them back empty. The disciples fished all night, but they didn't catch a single fish.

Early the next morning, a man waved to them from the shore. The man shouted, "Catch anything?"

The fishermen yelled back, "No!"

Then the man called, "Drop your nets on the right side of the boat, and you'll find some fish."

Peter grumbled, "Here we work all night and don't catch a thing, then some wise guy thinks we'll find fish on the other side of the boat."

Thomas and John untangled the nets. The men balanced themselves carefully as they threw out the huge nets on the right side of the boat.

Immediately, fish started
flopping in the nets. The nets became
so full that some fish flipped back out
and swam away.

John looked at the loaded nets and
said, "The man we obeyed is Jesus."

Peter jumped out of the boat and swam toward the shore. The other disciples guided the boat back to land, dragging the heavy nets behind them.

Jesus had already started a fire on the beach.

"Bring some of the fish you caught," Jesus directed.

This time, Peter obeyed Jesus without grumbling. He dragged one of the nets onto the beach.

One hundred fifty-three very large fish
were flopping in the nets.

Jesus invited, "Come and eat breakfast."

The disciples obeyed again. They wanted
to follow Jesus in every way.

After school the next day, Cole settled at the piano as his friends' voices floated in from outside.

"Hey, Keyboard Cole," Jason yelled through the window. "Aren't you coming?"

"I'll be out at 4:45," Cole said and banged the window shut.

Knock. Knock. Knock. Jason came to the door.

"Your mom will never know if you practice inside or play outside," Jason said.

"But *I* will," Cole explained. "If I don't follow the rules, I feel bad."

"Leave him alone, Jason," Amanda said. "Cole's doing the right thing."

"Gotcha," said Kate, sneaking up to snatch Jason's cap.

"Hey," yelled Jason, turning to chase after her.

"I'll be out soon," Cole said with a smile. "At 4:45."

Children, obey your parents as the Lord wants, because this is the right thing to do.
—Ephesians 6:1 NCV

Flying Lunches

A Story about Friendship

It was almost noon when the five students puffed up the hill to the zoo picnic area.

"I'm starved," Jason announced as he began rummaging through the lunch bags.

"Jason," called Mrs. Meyer, "since you're already into the lunches, you can hand out the bags."

"I'm really just looking for mine," Jason muttered. He had had an awful morning. T. J., the new student, was not only smart, but everyone accepted him as if they had all been friends forever.

Jason angrily tossed the bags to his classmates.

"Here's the new kid's bag," snapped Jason, as the bag sailed high into the air.

T. J. jumped, but the bag flew beyond his outstretched hand. Dismayed, he ran to see where his lunch had gone.

"Squawk, squawk, squawk."

A flurry of feathers pointed to the landing site. Ducks and geese waddled over to inspect the foreign objects.

"Now look what you've done," Amanda scolded as she turned to face Jason. "What's T. J. going to eat?"

"Come on," Cole said. "I'll share."

"I'll share, too," said Amanda.

T. J. smiled his thanks while Cole marched over to Jason, who was busy munching.

"What are *you* sharing?" Cole demanded.

"Huh?" Jason asked, getting ready to
take a big bite of his sandwich.

"What are *you* giving T. J.?" Cole repeated. "Remember
the story we heard at church about friends?"

"Oh, yeah," Jason mumbled, chewing as he remembered.
"The roof guys."

"Whoops!" Eli was so excited, he almost tripped over his own feet. He was in a hurry to tell his friend the big news.

"Jonas, Jesus is in town!" Eli called out.

Jonas looked up through tired eyes.

"Jesus is in town," Eli repeated. "Jesus can heal you!"

"I can't get to where Jesus is," Jonas said, smiling weakly. Jonas had been unable to walk for a very long time. If only Jesus could heal him!

"We will carry you," Eli said firmly. "We'll pick up your bed and take you to Jesus." Then Eli raced to get his friends.

When Eli returned, the four men carefully carried Jonas to the house where Jesus was teaching.

The crowd was so large, it overflowed out the door. The men could not even hear Jesus speak.

"This will not work," Jonas observed. "Thank you, my friends, but I can't even crawl through that crowd."

Then Eli had an idea. Scrambling up to the roof, he signaled his friends from the top.

"We can take off part of the roof," Eli said. "Then we can lower Jonas down to Jesus."

Carefully, the four friends carried Jonas on his bed up the stairs. Panting and sweating, they finally reached the roof. Cautiously, Eli started removing pieces of the roof.

"Whoops!" Eli said with a friendly wave, as dirt floated down on the richly dressed men below.

At last, the opening was large enough for the bed.

Slowly the four men lowered Jonas into the room below. Shouts and laughter floated up as the crowd watched Jonas enter through the roof.

Jesus smiled up at the men who were such good friends to Jonas. Then Jesus healed Jonas. Eli was so excited, he almost fell through the hole in the roof.

"Jonas, Jesus healed you!" The men rejoiced with their friend.

"Yes," cried Jonas. "But I wouldn't even be here if it weren't for my friends. I am grateful to Jesus and thankful for you."

Jason got up from the picnic table. Walking toward the group, he slid a small bag of cookies across the table to T. J.

"I'm full," Jason said.

"Thanks, Jason," T. J. said, shoving the cookies back across the table. "But I'm full, too. My friends gave me a big lunch."

Jason looked down at the cookies.

". . . wanted to share," he mumbled.

"Well, then, these will be a great snack for the trip home," said T. J. He examined the bag, then looked up with a broad smile. "I counted. There are just enough for each of us to have one."

"All set, group?" Cole asked.
"Lead on!" T. J. answered for everyone.

A friend loves you all the time.
            —Proverbs 17:17 NCV